D1073605

MODERN STAINED GLASS IN BRITISH CHURCHES

SAINT BARTHOLOMEW'S CHURCH, BATH
EAST WINDOW (Detail)
ARTIST: Mark Angus, 1981
The Cross: pain, suffering, the broken spirit. But purple, as a combination of red and blue, symbolizes Christ's shed blood and the power of the spirit — the resurrection implicit in the Crucifixion.

MODERN STAINED GLASS IN BRITISH CHURCHES

Mark Angus

Foreword by
JOHN PIPER C.H.

MOWBRAY
LONDON & OXFORD

ERRATA

The publishers regret the mis-spelling of Patrick
Reyntiens's name on pp. 32, 60, 111–115, and 120,
and the omission of his name on p. 114 as
co-designer with John Piper of the Lantern window
in the Cathedral of Christ the King in Liverpool.

British Library Cataloguing in Publication Data
Angus, Mark
    Modern stained glass in British Churches
    1. Glass painting and staining—Great Britain
    2. Church decoration and ornament—Great Britain
    I. Title
748.592   NK5343
    ISBN 0264 66986 X (hardback)
    ISBN 0 264 66964 9 (paperback)

Phototypeset by Oxford Publishing Services, Oxford
Printed in Great Britain by Cowells Ltd. of Ipswich

To Ann, Alexander and Beatrice

FOREWORD

IT WAS first pointed out to me, in Herbert Read's fine book *English Stained Glass* (1926), that stained glass, old or new, can be, and should be, *judged* — not just recorded. He says 'the aesthetic laws which distinguish it from other arts contemporary with it, and which are essential to its appreciation, are ignored to a degree unknown to the more familiar arts of architecture and painting.'

In the half century since he wrote this the situation has improved quite a lot. There was a big leap in the right direction after the Second World War, when so many churches in northern Europe were built or rebuilt and the demand for contemporary glass to complete and enhance contemporary churches (good and bad) was dramatically increased. Glass artists were forced to look hard at the buildings they were asked to adorn and therefore to adapt and relate their craft in an uncommonly strict way to the fountain-heads of architecture, painting and sculpture, instead of producing stock products of self-expression.

Mark Angus, whose book I welcome, has grown up in this age and has noticed (not to say marked and learned) that stained glass can be as integral and essential a part of a modern building as it was at Chartres and Canterbury. He has real beliefs about the subject and he *judges*, which Herbert Read would have approved of. So would Ruskin.

John Piper

5

Contents

ACKNOWLEDGEMENTS

My sincere thanks go to:

Peter Burman and his staff at the Council for the Care of Churches for their great help and encouragement;

John Piper for his help and for kindly writing the Foreword;

Professor Johannes Schreiter for his generous kindness;

Kenneth Baker of Mowbrays for his encouragement and kindness;

All the artists, architects, priests and vicars, churchwardens and others who have assisted me with information, answered my queries, found keys and helped in all manner of other ways, including Dr P. Baelz, Brother Bead, Ray Bradley, the Revd J. Brockbank, Jon Callan, the Revd John Carden, Angela Cartwright, Harry Cohen, the Revd S. Cunnane, F. Ellison, Harry Fairhurst, Alfred Fisher, the Revd E. Furness, Jane Gray, Amber Hiscott, the Revd Roger Hoare, Anthony Holloway, Catrin Jones, Christine Kirby, David LeVersha, the Revd John Luke, Penelope Neave, Graham Pentelow, the Revd A. Siddal, the Revd D. Swan, Brother Gilbert Taylor, David Wilson.

Bath, April 1983   MARK ANGUS

(All photographs are by the author except page 37, David Wilson, and page 103, the Revd Roger Hoare.)

Preface

EARLY ON, my interest in art tended towards those artists who used full and flat areas of colour, Matisse, Barnett Newman, Léger among others, yet strangely, I did not involve myself in painting, print making or other mediums that rely strongly on full colour. Equal to my enjoyment of strong intense colour was my interest in architecture. Drawing interested me when I was young, but technical and geometrical drawing fascinated me; preparing elevations and isometric projections was pleasure, not work. My interest with volumes and awareness of spaces within buildings caused me to read a lot of architecture books, preferably liberally illustrated ones. So I read about Le Corbusier, Bauhaus, Mies van der Robe, Frank Lloyd Wright and Charles Rene MacKintosh. My first art class was to study sculpture. At that time I think I would have tried to become an architect but I lacked the entry qualifications, as I did for town planning. I did eventually qualify as a chartered surveyor, an allied profession.

My first professional post was in Canterbury, and it was there that I had my first spiritual shock. The beautiful stained glass at Canterbury Cathedral is happily situated quite low down and by standing on a pew one can actually touch the glass in some windows. Straightaway it was the 'glassiness' of hand-made glass that arrested my imagination. I knew immediately that the material was beautiful and that I wanted to have hand-made glass with me, to look at, handle, touch and work. I recognized that this was pure colour, light direct into the eye, very powerful *and* that it could be used by itself architecturally and that it had modern application.

Obtaining my first glass determined my future. Although it was several years before I studied architectural stained glass at art school, that decision was inevitable from that first day in Canterbury. Equally inevitable was the decision, upon completion of the art school training, to establish myself as an artist designer of stained glass in my own studio at Bath.

Over that period I had learnt that there was good *modern* stained glass, but that for the most part it wasn't being made in the established business workshops. I began to look at the work of independent stained glass artists in this country and abroad, and to meet them and discuss their work with them. Among the artists whose work interested me were, in Germany, Johannes Schreiter, Ludwig Schaffroth, Wilhelm Buschulte, Georg Meisterman and Hubert Spierling, and in Britain the group of artists who came to public prominence in the 1960s, and who include John Piper, Keith New, Lawrence Lee and Margaret Traherne. Works by all these artists exist in modern and

9

older buildings, and some are illustrated in this book. However, there is now in Britain a new generation of independent artists whose art has in my eyes contemporary relevance, architectural understanding and aesthetic qualities that are new and worthy of public interest.

To some extent my own experiences have been shared by others. As my own powers to use the medium of glass develop, I also find the need to express the over-burgeoning ideas in other media. Currently, this includes drawing and painting, collage and print making. But central to my work is the need for it to have a relevant content and to be compatible with the architecture in which it is going to exist.

My hope is that this book will cause artists, church officials, architects and the 'person in the pew' to think hard about the function of architectural art in the church, and to use the power of glass positively for the better service of God and man.

M. A.

MODERN STAINED GLASS
IN BRITISH CHURCHES

SAINT ANDREW'S CHURCH, WHITEMORE REANS, WOLVERHAMPTON
WEST WINDOW (Detail)
ARTIST: John Piper

1. Twentieth century breakthrough

IT IS NOW over twenty years since the consecration of Coventry Cathedral in 1962. The large scale use of modern glass integrated into the whole building is a brilliant feature of the architecture. The originality of the stained glass at Coventry was the cause of controversy at the time, but it is now accepted as a landmark of British stained glass design. A barrier had been broken through, the old established traditions were forfeit. For several years after Coventry it looked again as if British stained glass would blossom anew into a full movement. With a few exceptions that momentum halted, and the revival never really came.

The new generation of glass artists has looked hard at the British glass tradition, and has increasingly looked abroad for inspiration and stimulus, notably to Germany, where the only true post-war stained glass movement has existed. Learning from these experiences, serious British artists are now attempting to develop the philosophies studied in a uniquely British way, a way that is relevant to the British character, climate and architecture. This has involved a reassessment of the immediate British past as well as the present day spiritual needs.

This book does not attempt to analyse the reason for the failure of the British artist in the 1960s to sustain the momentum, but looks at the glass art which is being produced today for the church, and at what the author believes are healthy signs for a recovery in stained glass in Britain. That recovery may be assisted by an increasing secular use of stained glass integrated into new, more tactile architecture. But although the content of a design may vary if the artist is working for the church or a secular building, the criterion of high aesthetic standards, an awareness of the function of the building as well as the role of art work within the space, and the spiritual quality of light will remain the same. This book does not make a case for a particular style, rather that individual artists should be able to respond to the spiritual needs of today's society in a relevant and contemporary way. The author would subscribe to the motto 'art for architecture' but would greatly prefer as a prerequisite 'spirituality in art'!

SAINT MARY THE VIRGIN, CLAVERTON, AVON
MARK HIBBERD MEMORIAL WINDOW
ARTIST: Mark Angus, 1983
'I will lift up mine eyes unto the hills'

2. Spiritual quality of light

And God said, Let there be light: and there was light. And God saw the light that it was good: and God divided the light from the darkness. (FIRST DAY OF CREATION)

THE JEWISH religion understood the spiritual quality of light, but it was the Christian Church that used coloured light in stained glass windows knowing its spiritual quality. The artists, architects and craftsmen who created Augsberg, St Denis, Chartres, Notre-Dame and Canterbury lived in an age of certainty, an age of total faith and total acceptance. Spectacular stained glass was used by the Church to express the glory of God, using rich jewelled effects. This created the environment and the atmosphere suitable for the worship of God, a sensual atmosphere that made man more receptive to God. For the ordinary illiterate man this must have seemed a miracle, a magical world, and the images accepted as truth, for life was closely interwoven with the supernatural. The stained glass would have given a visual meaning to the Word of God contained in the Bible. Like a modern day cartoon strip, these windows would have been the 'poor man's Bible'.

The subject matter of these early windows illustrated in a literal, figurative form Old and New Testament stories and characters. Old and New Testament figures (type and anti-type) the lineage of Christ, pictures of saints, miracles and events were all favourite subject matter. The effect created awe and splendour and illustrated a triumphant God. The Church was powerful, the congregation largely illiterate. Elsewhere the use of imagery was much less than today. The holy theatre must have seemed magical and mysterious.

The Victorian age was an age of progress, an age of growth, industry, the steam engine. It was also an age of known security and confidence. In stained glass the symbolism and subject matter was equally clear. Gothic, which had become almost synonymous with Christian architecture, needed an easily understood symbolism. Apart from illustrating particular saints and prophets, favourite subjects were the life of Christ and other biographical scenes, and the virtues and such like. Although they have more vitality than eighteenth century art, these works look to the modern eye languid, over-pious and sentimental. But such is the hold that this style has on some parts of British opinion that production of these now uninspired and irrelevant works sadly continues. Art must be alive, and the artist with integrity who is committed uncompromisingly to his work must be encouraged and allowed to develop. The traditional relationship of patron and artist that has existed between the Church is essential both to the Church and to the artist. The Church should provide the opportunity and the encouragement, the artist the daring and vision.

During this century the Church has largely ignored contemporary art and has made use of second rate 'art' that harked back to the past. Yet, at the same time, contemporary church architecture and liturgy has liberated itself from traditional forms and ornament. There has been a desire for light and space, simplicity and order. Art has rightly become part of the worship rather than the decoration of the church building. There is a great deal of work for the artist in the church, for artists designing and making articles of liturgical use (candlesticks, cross, crucifix, etc.) painting and the more architectural sculpture, stained glass, the altar and other furnishings. The contemporary Church should have a living art which not only expresses and reflects religious life, but ennobles and strengthens everyday life. The Church cannot offer the twentieth century the image it offered the nineteenth century. It must have its moment of ecstasy if it is to live in the twentieth century. The artist and the Church will be strengthened by the contribution of each other.

Our age can be called the age of science, the atomic age. Science has assumed a new and powerful importance in our lives. Scientists can account for so many 'mysteries' in scientific terms. Technology is now a master and determines much in our society. Victorian sentimentality is out of place here. And yet, paradoxically, the Victorians' known security is no longer felt. Man no longer fears plague as in the Middle Ages, but he has the technology to destroy himself and this planet, and/or to explore the universe. Equally, in architecture, man has the ability to build brutalistic megastructures that dominate and dwarf the human spirit, or he can build architecture that has spirit, spacial and tactile qualities and grace that qualify to rank with man's greatest achievements.

What can the present-day architectural artist say in his work that is relevant to today? More particularly, when in service to the Church what can the artist say that is spiritually relevant to humanity?

16

3. New focus in a technological age

'That which from the beginning, which we have heard, which we have seen with our eyes, which we have looked upon and touched with our hands, concerning the word of life'. (1 JOHN 1. 1)

ART WITH its sense of wonder can assist the mystical. It is not just the intellect but all the senses — eyes, ears, touch, smell and taste — through which religion stimulates. Art can express an extra dimension of religion, and an increased sensitivity towards it can assist in realizing our wholeness. Spiritual experiences come in different forms; for some in music, for others in architecture. For some the experience is in nature or relationships, or sexual joy, for others in worship or the spoken word of holy theatre. To the visually aware the experience may be in the effect of coloured light. The Christian Church has always used the visual, whether as movements or as images, as a way of enriching faith and understanding. It is right and proper that the modern Church expresses itself through art in a relevant and contemporary way. In fact it is essential.

The function of art in the Church has changed radically since the Middle Ages. The 'poor man's Bible' is no longer relevant to an intelligent congregation able to read. Today we are bombarded at home, at work, in the street and at recreation with visual instructions (road signs, etc.) persuasion (advertisements, etc,) and entertainment (television, video, books, etc.). The function of today's architectural art in churches should rather be to create the atmosphere (passive or charged) to emphasize architectural focal points (e.g. altar, lectern, pulpit) to contain the eye and mind and control the light. These might be described as architectural or environmental functions, enabling the concentration on worship and awareness of God. But, more importantly, the work must relate specifically to the function of the building. It must express faith in a spiritual and theological way with originality and distinction that is relevant to today's needs.

The advances of knowledge and understanding should make our times an age of expanding horizons. One would expect this to be reflected in the subject matter artists dare to handle. In fact this increased knowledge of man's place in the universe may have assisted in challenging artists to risk subjects such as the creation, light out of darkness, growth, the elements etc., but it is more likely that the acceptance and power of the abstract image combined with the artist's wish to address himself to the fundamental meanings behind such things as martyrdom, or the sacraments, has brought this change about. Equally, there has been an understandable tendency not to tackle subjects such as, for example, scenes from the life of Jesus, in any representative way.

The modern artist is not so concerned with the historical events and what figures may have looked like or how they dressed, rather he is very interested in the relationships, the emotions and passions, relating these to his experience of life. This is a deliberate change of focus designed to illustrate an ancient truth in a way that can be understood in today's terms. So again, it is unlikely, for example, that the crucifixion will be portrayed as Jesus the man in pain and suffering on the cross, powerful though this image would be. Instead the truth that the historical event symbolizes, that through pain, suffering and sacrifice is the wonder of the resurrection; that paradox of opposing forces brings the historical event into our daily lives with renewed force.

Art is not inferior to philosophy as a way of knowing and seeing; in particular, when defining, yet maintaining mystery, art has an ambiguity and necessary indirectness. Art can juxtapose opposing or unrelated images in a unique and shattering way. Stained glass with its intrinsic spirituality and direct power can be used positively to stimulate the senses and challenge the intellect. Art can also give the viewer the sense of being part of something greater than oneself and at the same time art in a church can arouse the soft maternal world, a sense of being protected and sheltered. The power of stained glass can stir up and move the viewer and give a sense of the distant past and far into the future.

4. Modern expressions of symbolism

BECAUSE THE modern artist is independent and may work for the Church and galleries and private patrons during his life, there has been pressure to assert that an artist's work is measured only to the degree to which the work exposes his personal philosophy. When it is argued that the artist has to have 'integrity' and be 'uncompromising' these terms are sometimes used to describe the degree in which the artist expresses his ideas in his unique way, his line, his use of colour, tone and texture. This is unmodified by the function of the building, the situation in the building and the relative importance of the work. When the artist is painting an autonomous canvas there may be a degree of truth in this argument. When the artist is creating a work for an architectural situation, and especially when the building is a church, the argument is fallacious. Pure aesthetics is, although a subjective decision, one factor in the success of an architectural work, but only one factor among many. Most important of these factors is the spiritual content of a work which is concerned with the mysteries of faith. Equally important are the other factors inside the Church — the *genius loci*; no art work should be designed in isolation and ignoring the context in which it will be seen.

It is preferable that the artist expresses himself clearly so that the meaning of his work is communicated, rather than that the work is solely drawn well or is a slick but hollow resolution to a design problem. I would rather see a powerful content that stirred me than a well drawn angel that lacked the power of touching my thoughts. Those who argue that the content or the subject matter is the wrong criterion by which to judge a work for the Church, are mistaken, in my opinion. Art without a specific Christian content can make no relevant contribution to the church building. Alongside that statement, I would add that works that possess inherited symbols and signs, but lack the power to illuminate the vision of the searching contemporary artist, and works that imitate dead art are equally an irrelevant contribution to the Church. This is not, however, to say that these artists lack sincerity or they are incapable of genuine Christian experience.

The traditional understanding of religion is that it gives us humanly significant values and symbols. This contrasts with science which traditionally is restricted to facts relating to the physical universe. However, the immense growth of technology and the prestige with which it is held, combined with the now known vastness of the universe that science has shown us, has given technology and science something of a religious awe. Jung described unidentified flying objects as technological angels, having mysterious origins and marvellous freedom. Science, here symbolized in the imagination by UFOs, has become an envoy of cosmic life and is held on a scale equal to great religions of the past.

Clearly, we are still desperate to experience wonder, and those theologians who have concentrated on the moral and existential 'core' of religion have produced a faith with no sense of transcendence and wonder. The modern man, who is scientifically educated, may have difficulty in accepting the ascension of Jesus, angelic visitations, or miracles in the literal way that medieval man accepted them. The artist can respond to this difficulty in perhaps two ways. Firstly, he can develop new symbols and visual language to express the wonder and joy he feels, to express himself in the unique way of colour and line, to communicate what it is impossible to say in any other medium, words, music or action. The imagery may be derived from the artist's love for nature, landscape, people, music, architecture, but will be intended to communicate a fundamental of faith, the mystery and majesty in a new way.

Alternatively, the artist may use technology itself as his subject matter, the set-square and ruler, the machine line. If the artist can interpenetrate into this approach an accessible awareness of the presence of God in our daily lives, then the approach can succeed. If not, the results will be a cold, threatening and God-less hybrid with no spiritual qualities.

Through history, styles have changed. At any one point in time many styles will exist, although since many experiences of an age are those of its artists, this will unify overall philosophies. Each artist can only show a part of the truth, but if that part is illuminating in its time, then it is valid. Styles change, and with the change we see different aspects of the same truth. This is an important process as it constantly refreshes and stimulates. The perspective of history will allow us to know which periods succeeded in creating relevant art, but each generation has a duty to attempt to add to the knowledge of the past. This is a duty which we have to ourselves and to our successors.

The early Christian artists used signs and symbols, shorthand presentations which communicate quickly. If these are known to the viewer, they are useful. For example the symbol of a fish means Jesus Christ; as a car sticker it means 'I am a Christian'. The halo or nimbus indicates divinity or holiness. They are useful conventions, but they do not illuminate. They are moribund

An example of Ludwig Schaffrath's work at St Antonius Hospital Chapel, Eschweiler, West Germany: One of six windows, 1976

symbols in art as they do not show the essence of holiness, they do not illustrate the underlying meaning of what they symbolize.

The modern artist must communicate what is spiritual and not what is material. He may use the material in realistic, representative or abstract form, but as a vehicle for expressing the spiritual. Abstract art is more powerful than figurative art, if the artist is trying to express spiritual ideas. Each generation of artists must develop its own symbolism to serve its own times. The artist who has command of that visual language provides a force for the Christian Church to use. The attainment of representative truth in British church art has been replaced by a new language that has reasserted religious awe and wonder in a way that no number of pious painted saints would do.

Ours must be a pilgrim church, it needs boldness, courage and faith to move to the future. So we must seek to develop and understand the symbolism and meaning of today's work. We are being offered new dimensions intended to meet the needs of the new congregation. The sense of the holy within a church is obtained when the holy theatre of worship fuses with the symbolism and meaning of art which, together, speak to *all* the senses.

5. Directions, influences, applications

TRAVEL TODAY has cut down the distances between places. It is now as easy to travel to Germany or America as it is to cross Britain. It is not surprising to find that artists with their thirst for experiences and truth travel across the world and form ties with new friends wherever they go. In many fields of art, communications are now so rapid that national styles rapidly become international. But whereas philosophies may be in common, applications will have to take local conditions and sensitivities into reckoning. National and local differences based on history, climate, character etc. will influence trends.

It is undeniable that in the post-war period the major achievements in stained glass design have been made in West Germany. The considerable variety of styles suggest that one should not refer to a modern 'German School' of stained glass, although there are stylistic similarities in the leading German artists' work. Because of a studio system that employs independent artists, German glass has been constantly revitalized by inputs of new creativity and has not perpetuated a particular style. Furthermore, the artists employed generally work in a number of fields simultaneously and are, therefore, more closely in touch with the mainstream fine arts.

The intensified spiritual context of differing qualities of hand-blown glass, reamy, opalescent, opaque and streaky, have given new internal and external opportunities for controlling light containing space and expressing ideas.

British and American students have noted these distinguishing features, and upon their return home have resolved to distance themselves from the established stained glass studios. They have recognized the need to remain rounded, innovative and independent artists working in as many fields as possible, while developing the specific areas of interest such as stained glass. This has led to the development of the studio artist working not as a member of a team but as an individual expressing himself through his art, and working in isolation in his studio. This phenomenon has taken place in other spheres, for example in hot glass and blacksmith artists.

In an excess of zeal some artists, wishing to emulate the German experience, have adopted German styles, particularly the more austere geometric, constructionist styles, especially in America. However, there has now been time to sieve the experiences and more serious British artists are developing a distinctive personal aesthetic move related to British needs.

An example of David Wilson's work at Church of Saint Thomas More, Cherryhill, New Jersey, USA: Passage Window, 1980 (Architects: Geddes, Brecher, Quails and Cunningham)

AN EXAMPLE OF CONTEMPORARY ART FROM WEST GERMANY

The church of St Marien in Dortmund was severely damaged during the Second World War and all the original glass destroyed. However, the beautiful altar painting of 1420 by Konrad von Soest was preserved and this still forms the focal point in the apse of the whole church. It was felt inappropriate to put further paintings behind this beautiful masterpiece. In 1969 Johannes Schreiter started designing for all thirty-three windows of the church. The windows are an aesthetic play of light and colour and they contain an expression of Christian faith in the abstract speech of modern man.

The artist, Johannes Schreiter says:

'To integrate contemporary art into a centuries-old structure is as risky as it is challenging. In the Marienkirche, Dortmund, the task to be solved was doubly difficult as it already presents in itself the tensions which arise from the conjunction of two differing architectural styles. Nave and towers are Romanesque; chancel and aisle, however, are High Gothic. In the creation of the 33 windows my aim was, in the first instance, to unify the two different architectural styles of chancel and nave through the basic elements of my design without detracting from the characteristic distinctions of these unique component parts. Therefore, all the windows, with the exception of one small Romanesque one in the southern aisle, contain the same vertical textural screen, varied to artistic necessity.

The principal parts of the design are the dark brown vertical beams comparable to the widths of the stone mullions, and large hanging areas of whites and organically formed departures from the stereotyped pale grey textured screens. It is above all these informal breaks in the surface uniformity which enter into a dialectic contrast to the building and illustrate the unpredictable, the unforeseen. Through these it becomes possible for the observer to relate the spiritual with human experiences.

The non-transparency of the glass makes a vital contribution for it contains the eye within the building, removing all the established facts in the physical realm of perceptibility. No detail of the outside world disturbs the challenge to transcend the "signals" of the windows.'

The emphasis on the vertical plane uses the religious metaphor of below and above. Every line strives upwards, becoming a pointer to the creator, God. The earthly congregation, symbolized in the liturgical colour red in the lower sections of the apse windows, has its counterpart in the upper sections of those windows. The lines that connect them are in places torn with chaotic deformations, an expression of the condition of present day humanity, the reality of sin. The windows try in a quiet way to bestow onto thinking and considering man the destructive effect of sin and what God does towards atonement and healing in his world.

Saint Marienkirche, Dortmund, West Germany. (Artist: Johannes Schreiter, 1972)

Saint Marienkirche, Dortmund, West Germany. Artist: Johannes Schreiter

6. Creative collaboration: patron and artist

WHEN commissioning new art work for the Church, it is essential that the brief be kept fairly open as to the content of the work and yet, at the same time, be fairly explicit. The artist must have freedom in which to work and yet know that his work is along agreed lines. The discussion process prior to the commencement of the actual design should be a creative relationship between the artist and the church. The content of the design will be governed by the needs of the church and the liturgical importance of the work. The artist, a visitor to the church called in for this specific purpose, will need the guidance of those who use the church perhaps daily, but can have the detachment and originality of vision that an outsider often has.

A design is only a suggestion, a graphic image rather than an artist's impression of an, as yet, unmade work. The design incorporates the content ideas, but the aesthetic art work lies in the making of the actual work. The artist must be allowed to expand and explore the image in its creation. The less final the design work, the better and more successful the experience of creating the actual work.

The creative collaboration where the church and artist contribute towards the eventual work, each from their own experience and expertise, will assist understanding between the parties, and does not restrict the artist. The process will need to be expanded to include the architect in many cases, especially in new buildings. Understanding will in turn lead to mutual trust, for successful works must involve risks.

The commissioning of an art work will be a growing process for church and artist, each understanding better the other's needs. The new addition to the church will stimulate interest in different directions. If the new window or whatever can bring about links in other directions, the church is doubly richer. An example I can give of this is a church near me which linked a new window with the Amnesty International Movement. An element in the design was the spark for the link, and it has given a whole new meaning and significance to the work, a bonus that was unforeseen by artist and church alike, but welcomed by both.

No matter how the opportunity arises whereby a new art work is commissioned, be it for architectural reasons such as an excess of glare, or the gift of money, or the spiritual needs of a congregation, the artist must always spend time in the building absorbing how it functions, analysing how it works. In some cases (and always in new buildings) the opportunity can be taken to

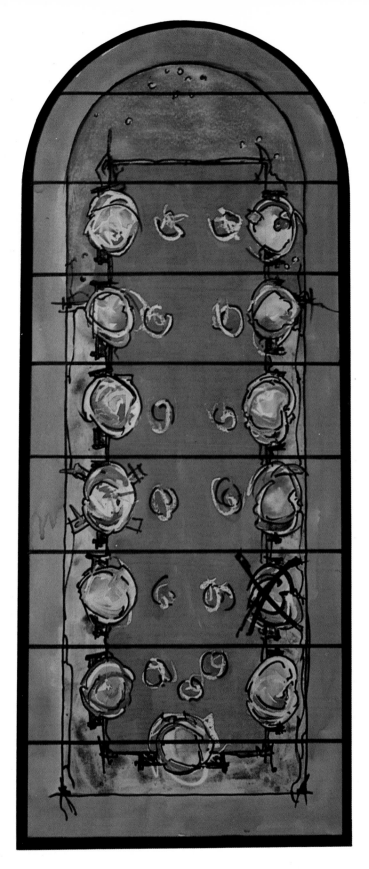

Design for a Stained Glass Window, North Aisle, Durham Cathedral. Theme: Transformation — Physical and Spiritual Food; the Last Supper. (Artist: Mark Angus, 1983)

prepare schemes for the whole of a building, determining parameters of light values, colour intensities, etc. Liturgical and theological advice is usually freely given and is invaluable to the artist. The artist must always bear in mind that his work is experienced daily by ordinary people. His work's meaning must be accessible, explain mystery, and yet maintain mystery, give insight and meaning alongside awe.

The author believes that the searching artist in stained glass can attempt these objectives briefly outlined in this essay, and now invites the reader to study the illustrations. If the photographs give a fraction of the joy, wonder, warmth and meaning that many of these works have given the author, he will be satisfied. If it prompts the reader to seek out or look again at contemporary glass known to him or her and to experience it in a new way the author will be more than satisfied.

ILLUSTRATED WORKS

List of Illustrated Works

ROBINSON COLLEGE CHAPEL, CAMBRIDGE

ARCHITECT: GILLESPIE KIDD AND COIA

CHANCEL WINDOW, 1978–80

ARTIST: JOHN PIPER

The new Robinson College is a large, intricate and very successful structure with interesting aspects, and at times beautiful brickwork. The attention to detail has been remarkable. At the centre of the college is the Ecumenical Chapel, which is distinguished by the fine art and craftsmanship employed.

The chapel does not follow usual design, having a very shallow nave. The chancel window is seen best as one enters and can see behind a hanging wall which partially obscures the window to the viewer in the pew. Taking as its theme the Light of the World, the window is rich in luscious detail and rich colours; a hanging garden that culminates in a bright sun at the top of the window. The effect is to create a lively atmosphere in this multi-purpose room, and yet still to focus attention on the altar. The window stimulates the senses fully and the viewer feels uplifted and refreshed.

ROBINSON COLLEGE CHAPEL, CAMBRIDGE

ANTE CHAPEL WINDOW, 1982

ARTIST: JOHN PIPER

At the entrance to the Robinson Chapel is a small antechapel. The room is very dark and still, contrasting totally with the Lady Chapel. Used for private meditation and prayer or quiet discussion with the chaplain, the room provides a valuable secret space with a very different function from the chapel itself.

The design is based on the Romanesque tympanum at Neuilly-en-Donjan, Allier. The original stone and now the window portrays the adoration of the Magi, flanked by trumpeting angels. Two green monsters, the beasts of paganism, are beneath their feet. The lower section depicts the beginning and the end of the Christian story; on the left are Adam, Eve and the serpent, and on the right is the Last Supper.

SAINT STEPHEN'S CHURCH, BATH

EAST WINDOW, LADY CHAPEL, 1983

ARTIST: MARK ANGUS

Known as the Centenary Window, having been commissioned to mark the church's first hundred years, the east window of the Lady Chapel is appropriately dedicated to St Stephen. The window opening is rather ugly plate tracery, but the glass design unifies the whole so that the viewer ceases to be aware of the stonework's lack of grace.

'The new East window to the Lady Chapel at St Stephen's, Bath, is designed on the theme of martyrdom, and the imagery attempts to depict *transformation*. The patron saint, St Stephen, is shown in transformation at the moment of his martyrdom. The idea of transformation is fundamental to Christian belief and to the design of the window. St Stephen is the vehicle for the theme.

The saint is seen on the bridge between life and death. The distorted, ambiguous body has elements of pain, yet the pose is calm and the saint raises his hand in forgiveness. The face in particular is transformed and is shown in pale grey as if disappearing. The whole body is lifting up, and this upward emphasis is strengthened by the hand, the martyr's palm, the head's orientation and the flames which rise in each of the three lancets. The red stones have moved back to form an arch and the blue behind the figure lifts it gently.

The work visually offers an insight into the subject in a relevant and contemporary way. The work retains the mystery of faith but is triumphant'.

Mark Angus, Artist

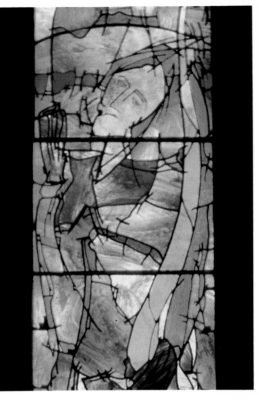

ALL SAINTS CHURCH, HABERGHAM, BURNLEY

EAST WINDOW, 1976

ARTIST: BRIAN CLARKE

All Saints Church, Habergham, Burnley, is a dismal, dark Victorian Gothic Church with a mediocre interior. The east window, installed in 1976 and replacing obscured diamond panes with a completely dead light provides a much needed focal point, transforming the interior, bringing new life and meaning.

The theme of the east window is creation with the elements of earth, water and sky. But, linked to this, the rainbow is a reminder of Noah, of judgement and promise and a new creation. The large green area at the base of the window gives stability to the composition and a dramatic contrast to the unsettling tilt of the rainbow.

SAINT ANDREW'S CHURCH, CUFFLEY

NORTH AND SOUTH AISLE WINDOWS, 1965, 1975

ARCHITECTS: CLIFFORD CULPIN AND PARTNERS

ARTIST: WHITEFRIARS STUDIO (Fifteen Aisle Windows)

CHAPEL STUDIO (South Aisle Window)

Saint Andrew's Church, Cuffley, was designed in 1965. It has an 'A' frame construction with recessed aisles with fifteen narrow slits. The church was awarded a Civic Trust Award in 1968 and remains an outstanding example of church design for that period.

The church is almost unique in having a complete integral series of fused glass windows. The technique involves heating glass pieces together in a kiln to form a single panel which glows with a rich intensity. There is currently a renewed interest in glass fusing and it is likely that in combination with more traditional techniques, it will be used more widely in the future, both in secular and non-secular architecture.

In 1975 it was decided to glaze the large window in the south aisle and opposite the choir, due to the disturbing level of glare.

'The colour was selected to give a restrained warm glow to this corner of the church while the simplest possible symbolism was employed, that of the tree of life merging with the life-giving source of the sun. The richest areas of colour form the tree'.

Alfred Fisher, Chapel Studios

SAINT ANDREW'S CHURCH, CUFFLEY

NORTH AND SOUTH AISLES

ARTIST: WHITEFRIARS STUDIO

The design of the fifteen aisle windows employs a gradation of colour from west to east. The layers of glass that are fused together without the need for connecting leads builds up a rich depth of colours. In a controlled design the effect can be very penetrating, evoking many positive responses from the viewer.

'The theme of the windows, "The earth is the Lord's and all that therein is" is conveyed solely by a sense of joy in the varying combinations of light and colour though the words of the text are concealed in the glass'.

Alfred Fisher, Artist

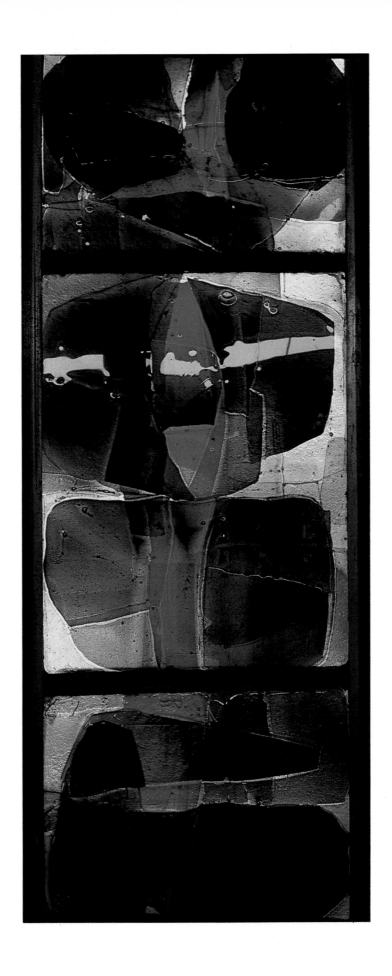

THE ABBEY OF SAINT MARY AND SAINT PETER, PRINKNASH

SCHEME OF DALLE DE VERRE WINDOWS

ARCHITECT: BROADBENT, HASTINGS, READ, AND TODD

ARTIST: BROTHER GILBERT TAYLOR

Prinknash Abbey is situated in hilly countryside near Painswick. It is a new complex of buildings. The church is glazed around with dalle-de-verre windows, a technique using one-inch thick glass cast in this case into resin. All the windows are designed and made on site by Brother Gilbert. The interior is dark which intensifies the quality of the colour. The designs are thematic, the Last Supper in the apse, symbols of Our Lady etc., but expressed in an abstract form. The red window illustrated is near the north entrance and denotes the dedication of the church, Our Lady and St Peter with the three keys and a pattern of Fleur-de-Lys. The whole effect is spectacular and very special, a spiritually rich atmosphere in which to worship.

CHURCH OF THE SACRED HEART, COVENTRY

ARCHITECTS: WILLIAMS AND WINKLEY

14 CIRCULAR WINDOWS, 1979–80

ARTIST: GODDARD AND GIBBS STUDIOS

The new church of the Sacred Heart, Coventry, was built alongside the existing church when that earlier church became too small for the growing congregation.

The use of stained glass though minimal, only fourteen small 'portholes', is refreshing and original, and indicates the continuing use by contemporary architects of the 'tactile' in their buildings. Indeed, this church would probably have benefitted from many more portholes of stained glass to define the altar area more clearly. The pulse of coloured circles could have been made to emanate from the heart of the altar, defining it as a source of energy and light, and focussing the worshipper on the altar. As it is, these interesting circles of colour do contribute a small measure of art to the building.

Apart from the limited use of stained glass, the architecture fails to produce the sense of wonder and distinctness necessary for a house of God. It has no sense of the holy. The brutalistic concrete blocks and concrete frame contrast with the articulated roof structure and 'green-house' roof to create a building largely undistinguishable from a modern warehouse or market building.

CHURCH OF ST PETER AND ST PAUL, ALDEBURGH

NORTH AISLE WINDOW BENJAMIN BRITTEN MEMORIAL WINDOW, 1979

ARTIST: JOHN PIPER

The flint and sandstone church of St Peter and St Paul looks down over Aldburgh and the sea. It is fitting that this church honours Benjamin Britten and that the artist was John Piper, a lifelong friend and collaborator of Britten. The lyrical window depicts Benjamin Britten's three parables for church performance; the Burning Fiery Furnace (1968), Curlew River (1964) and The Prodigal Son (1968). The Burning Fiery Furnace and The Prodigal Son are both stories from the Bible, but Curlew River is based upon a Japanese Noh play (Sumidagawa), and it is the Japanese tradition that forms the framework for each of the three 'Church Operas'. The Japanese origins of the Curlew River are beautifully echoed in the plant forms in the lower part of the central lancet.

SAINT LAWRENCE'S CHURCH, LONGRIDGE

GALLERY WINDOWS, 1975

ARTIST: BRIAN CLARKE

The small parish church of St Lawrence, Longridge, has a pair of galleries running the length of the nave and on each side, north and south. The lower nave windows contain fairly typical Hogan of Whitefriars windows which contrast with the new clerestory windows.

The subject matter of the clerestory windows is purely secular, being derived from local geographical features, and would not be out of place in a field study centre. It consists principally of reservoirs, local hills and quarries, and the meandering course of the River Ribble. Externally the simple Gothic window shapes are pleasantly emphasized by the opalescent glass borders. Internally, the windows are probably too dominant being so high up, but possess a beautiful feel for landscape. The large blue glass areas in particular are very evocative of the reservoirs that are close to the church. Whilst they are a beautiful addition to the church, the windows do not greatly enhance the special spiritual quality of it.

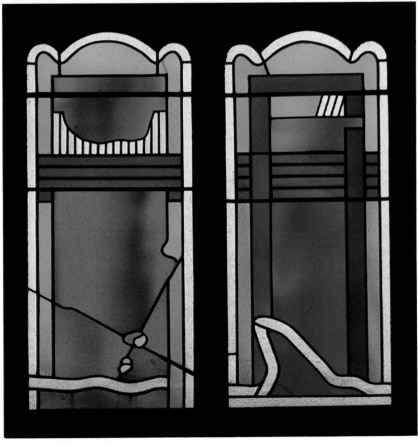

SAINT BARTHOLOMEW'S CHURCH, NETTLEBED

SOUTH AISLE WINDOW, 1976

ARTIST: JOHN PIPER

This window is a memorial to the explorer and traveller Peter Fleming. The design is a tree of life with exotic birds and an owl (as a writer for the *Spectator*, Peter Fleming used the pen name Stricks, which is the generic name for the owl). Additionally, the world and the heavens are shown in the top tracery light.

SAINT MARGARET'S CHURCH, TWICKENHAM

EAST AND BAPTISTRY WINDOWS, 1969

ARCHITECT: WILLIAMS AND WINKLEY

ARTIST: PATRICK REYNTIANS

When the image of an art object so much resembles a familiar object, it is difficult to understand what the artist is in fact saying. The modern church of St Margaret's is a light, airy building, internally of concrete blocks and excellently arranged, an adaptable and enjoyable architecture. The stained glass window set high over the altar in fact symbolizes Christ dispelling the darkness; the bright light, forcing the clouds rolling back, shines out. Once this theme is contemplated upon, the work has a depth of meaning.

60

SAINT ANDREW'S CHURCH, WHITEMORE REANS, WOLVERHAMPTON

ARCHITECTS: RICHARD TWENTYMAN AND PARTNERS

WEST WINDOW, 1968

ARTIST: JOHN PIPER

The modern church of St Andrew's replaces the old sandstone church which was destroyed by fire 1964. A feature of the church is the west window. As one enters the church, one is immediately aware of this being a special place. Blue light shines down through the stained glass window above one's head, and blue is reflected on the floor and reveals of the alcoved nave. A second wave of white daylight comes down through hidden windows high over the altar. Together this creates a warm feeling, a sensation of being in water looking upwards.

The large rectangular stained glass window over the west door is coloured in tones of the same blue and, in abstracted form, depicts a view of submarine sea life. During worship and with their backs to the window the congregation sense the work through reflected colour, yet have ample light by which to read. Upon turning, the window is first seen. Evocative of the patronal saint the design can be read on varying levels from the spiritual to the literal. It is surprisingly successful, given its simplicity of colour, and being non-figurative, wonderfully links the life of St Andrew back to early creation and forward to our own experiences of the sea.

CHURCH OF THE ENGLISH MARTYRS, HORNCHURCH

APSE AND NAVE WINDOWS, 1981

ARTIST: GODDARD AND GIBBS STUDIOS

The small estate Church of the English Martyrs was built in the early 1950s to cater for the needs of the expanding estates around Hornchurch. In 1981 the decision was made to develop a scheme of stained glass to fill the rectangular window openings. The first windows to be completed were those in the north aisle and they are appropriately dedicated to Thomas More and John Fisher. Later a window in the Lady Chapel was dedicated to St Mary. The groups of small windows which surround the apse take creation as their theme. These windows are brightly coloured, some in red, others in green or pink, and are rich with splendour and detail. The imagery is of early plants, and animal and bird life. There is a splendour in these works which succeeds in linking prehistory with today.

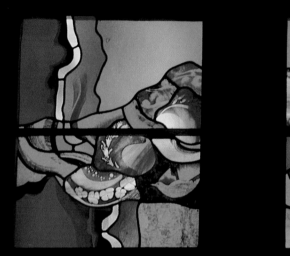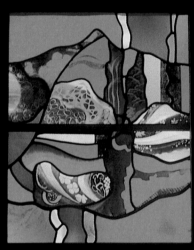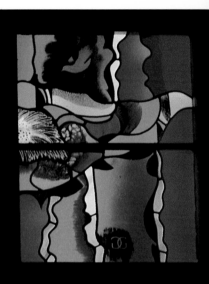

BIRCHOVER PARISH CHURCH, DERBYSHIRE

THREE SOUTH AISLE WINDOWS, 1977

ARTIST: BRIAN CLARKE

Set high in the Peaks, the little red sandstone village church at Birchover is a beautiful, small church set in breathtakingly wonderful stark countryside. Set against the side of the hill, the church has a nave with windows on just one side. The three windows (the gift of the artist) are delicately and softly coloured. Each window has four 'medallions', rectangles defined with opal white borders reminiscent in format of the medallions found in medieval stained glass. The simple window shapes are picked out and enhanced by a broken border ribbon. The imagery is evocative of the landscape; green below with spots of yellow and orange like spring flowers, and cold blues and whites above. The windows provide a gentle light, and are not too dominant, allowing the Victorian east window and altar to remain as the focal point of worship. Having little holding power of their own, the three aisle windows do create a passive mood in the church which facilitates a concentration on the act of worship.

SAINT PETER'S CHURCH, THUNDERSLEY

APSE WINDOWS, 1966

ARCHITECT: DONALD W. INSALL AND ASSOCIATES

ARTIST: RAY BRADLEY

Saint Peter's Church, Thundersley, is a large twentieth century structure added to a thirteenth century building in a unique and unusual combination. The old village church was too small to cope with the greatly increased population. So, in 1966, and with courage and imagination, the church was enlarged. The most attractive new church blends with the old and was awarded a Civic Trust Award in 1968.

The east end of the church has windows on the right and left that slope inwards as they rise. Due to this the congregation can only glimpse the stained glass, but the light flooding in throws colour reflections onto the white east wall. Both windows take as their theme St Peter, the Christian symbol of the Keeper of the Keys of the Kingdom of Heaven.

THE CATHEDRAL CHURCH OF SAINT MARY, SAINT DENYS AND SAINT GEORGE, MANCHESTER

THREE WINDOWS, WEST WALL, 1973, 1976, 1982

CATHEDRAL ARCHITECT: HARRY FAIRHURST

ARTIST: ANTHONY HOLLOWAY

'The Nave of the Cathedral was reglazed with uncoloured Norman slabs after bomb damage in 1940 which blew out every window. This gave a high level of lighting without colour.

When a donor offered a window in 1971 it seemed right to ensure that whatever was done was set in a context for the whole; to avoid random adornment then and in the future.

The Dean and Canons agreed to commission Anthony Holloway to study the whole building to establish a planning context for glass as a setting for the first window.

The gradual implementation of this concept as one window has followed another has allowed the artist's style to evolve and enhanced the visual interest and warmth of the building. This is particularly the case now that three contiguous windows exist. The Chapter, the Friends and the public have been thoroughly involved throughout. In 1983 design for a fourth window has been commissioned'.

Harry M. Fairhurst, Architect

Perhaps the most notable feature of the new stained glass at Manchester Cathedral is that it follows an exhaustive feasibility study into means of controlling the light within the building. This involved the making of a scale model with a scheme for the complete reglazing. The subject matter of each has not been predetermined. It seems right to me that the glazing be integrated into the architecture in a planned way so as to avoid the jumble of styles and approaches that can happen, always provided that the parameters of the overall plan allow sufficient artistic freedom for works of stature to be created in the future. The feasibility study should establish a conceptual framework; the artists who work towards realizing this wholeness will contribute their individuality and idiosyncrasies which will bring necessary richness and variation.

MANCHESTER CATHEDRAL

WEST WALL, SAINT MARY WINDOW, 1982

ARTIST: ANTHONY HOLLOWAY

The St Mary window has blue elements, the colour traditionally associated with the Virgin. A perfect circle has been broken by a Sword (. . .'and a sword shall pierce through your own soul also') and a serpent's head can also be perceived (. . .'it shall bruise your head and you shall bruise his heel').

The theme of the window is the Magnificat: and the words of the Magnificat are combined in the design:

> He that is mighty hath magnified me and holy is his name
> He hath put down the mighty from their seat
> And hath exalted the humble and meek
> He hath filled the hungry with good things
> And the rich he hath sent empty away

'The emergence of an image is not dependent upon the literary sources yet the forms may be set in motion in the imagination by the shapes and colours suggested during the research process.

The uppermost control within the design is that of the formal relationships of line colour, tone, texture and shape. A fine balance exists in my designs between the literary source as an inspiration for shapes, colour equations, and the entity of the design as a formal and dignified statement in conjunction with the architecture'.

Anthony Holloway, Artist

MANCHESTER CATHEDRAL

WEST WALL, SAINT DENYS WINDOW, 1976

ARTIST: ANTHONY HOLLOWAY

This window incorporates themes connected with St Denys of France, one of the cathedral patron saints. Included are the lions of Lorraine and an impression of the Basilique of Saint Sermin, the principal Roman Catholic church in Toulouse with which the cathedral entered a twinning in 1968, as an ecumenical venture. The window stands as an aspiration towards peace and unity.

SAINT EDMUND'S CHURCH, EDMONTON

SANCTUARY WINDOW, 1982

ARTIST: MARK ANGUS

The sanctuary window of St Edmund's, Edmonton, is the main source of light onto the altar. The idea of light itself became the theme for the glass design. Specifically the Easter Exultet provides the text around which the work was created:

'Accept this easter candle,
a flame divided but undimmed,
a pillar of fire that glows to the honour of God.
Let it mingle with the light of Heaven
and continue bravely burning
to dispel the darkness of this night!
May the Morning Star which never sets find this
flame still burning:
Christ, the Morning Star, who came back from the dead
and shed his peaceful light on all mankind,
your Son who lives and reigns for ever and ever'.

The pillar of fire becomes a laser beam; Christ cutting through everyday life. The sensation of the night sky lit up from the pillar of fire bringing light onto the earth is prominent.

SAINT EDMUND'S CHURCH, EDMONTON, LONDON

CHANCEL WINDOW, 1982

ARTIST: MARK ANGUS

Contrasting with fire in the sanctuary, the theme of water and baptism was adopted in this chancel window. The design links watery elements, and the font with the seven sacraments, emphasizing the positive blessings of Christ's Church.

HILLINGDON HOSPITAL CHAPEL, HILLINGDON

SCHEME OF 26 WINDOWS: 1965

ARTIST: JANE GRAY

In the heart of Hillingdon Hospital can be found the hospital chapel. The interdenominational chapel is used by staff, visitors and patients alike as a place for contemplation, for gaining spiritual strength as well as for more formal acts of worship. How much of an improvement to this special place it must have been when the twenty-six windows with their strong colour were completed. The artist here has developed a modern symbolism to express an old fundamental of faith in a relevant way.

'The chapel is interdenominational and was bleak; clear glass windows showed passers-by outside. My objective was to bring a message of hope, comfort and inspiration to anyone entering this hospital chapel who might be feeling apprehensive, desolate or joyful.

The images had to be satisfying and easily understood. I chose as my theme for the first thirteen windows Christianity entering the world of man. A spark of faith, represented by an ammonite, forms the centre. Each panel is 2 feet high by 4 feet wide so I let the observer's eye carry this image beyond its physical confines; an idea that is repeated elsewhere in the scheme as it allows for a change of scale in the subject matter. Flanking the prehistoric ammonite are two themes for today — Integration and Peace and War. In the former the colour is restrained. Vertical strips of tinted white glass meet horizontals of deep purple; colours and shapes merging in the centre: we can hope. In the latter I have echoed light and dark tones, keeping the lines of the dove softer than those of the hawk while setting them on a background of contrasting shapes.

The opposite wall also has a line of thirteen windows, and they carry an eternal message. The word of God bursts as from a seed pod, spreading far and wide. Once again the images, this time from the book of Revelation, have to be translated into impressions — one's eye accepts the arc of heaven; the seven-branched candlestick exists although only the candle flames are visible.

Hope, comfort and inspiration. The glass speaks for itself'.

Jane Gray, Artist

80

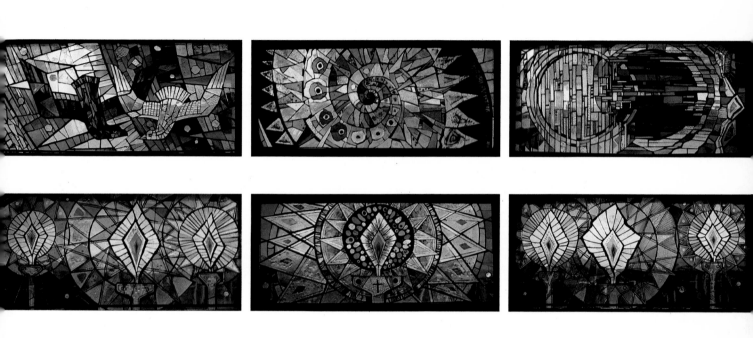

OUR LADY OF THE TAPER CHURCH, CARDIGAN

WEST WINDOW, 1980

ARTIST: AMBER HISCOTT

The west end at Our Lady of the Taper, Cardigan, is a glass wall. A strip of stained glass runs the length of the wall and depicts the sacraments in symbolic, contemporary forms which allow their theological meaning to be found. Altogether, there are twelve sections depicting baptism, confirmation, the Eucharist and, illustrated, the sacrament of reconciliation, holy orders, the anointing of the sick, and the sacrament of marriage, followed by eternal life.

'Our new life can be destroyed by sin (indicated by the break in the band of golden light) but is restored through the Sacrament of Reconciliation, symbolized by the free form opening out with new vigour.

Holy Orders is shown as a vineyard (Israel was God's vineyard, and Jesus said "I am the vine, you are the branches"); it is the disciplined cultivation of the garden of God.

The Anointing of the Sick which heals us in our bodies, souls and emotions is indicated by the general shape of a flower, conveying wholeness, and the use of green for healing and growth.

The Sacrament of Marriage is seen as a flower (nourished by the water of life) in which the bud, representing the child, is nestling in the protection of its parents. It is one of the great themes of the New Testament that the love of husband and wife is a symbol of the love between Christ and his Church.'

The Very Reverend S. Cunnane

SAINT DUNSTAN'S CHURCH, KEYNSHAM

WEST WINDOW, 1979

ARTIST: MARK ANGUS

With the use of purple to symbolize the hands of God, the contained form in the west window of St Dunstan's Church itself becomes a cross. God is thus portrayed holding the Church with the severn sacraments. Outside the purple areas are fiery red colours and elements of disorder and anarchy. The contrast in colour and articulation is appropriately pronounced.

   Seen from the outside the opalescent white cross reads clearly. Facing the main road and being above the church entrance this symbol is a prominent sign; an additional and useful function of the stained glass.

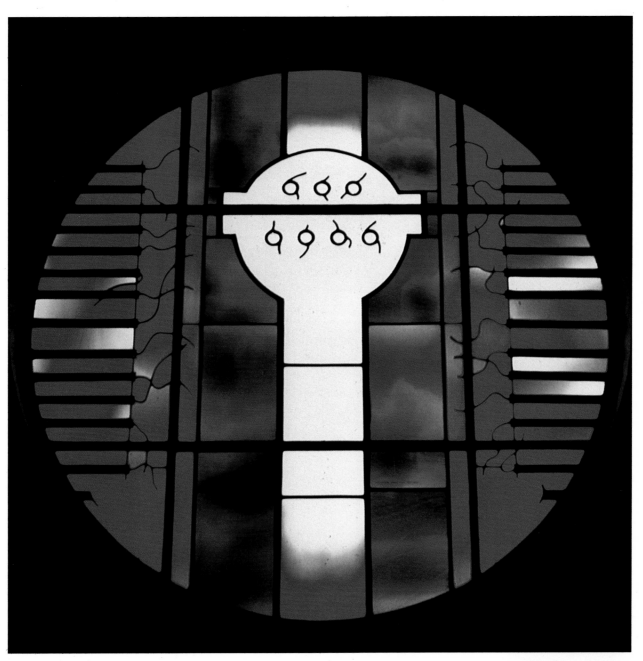

ALL SAINTS CHURCH, OYSTERMOUTH

SOUTH AISLE WINDOW, 1977

ARTIST: TIMOTHY LEWIS

In 1947 the entire crew of the Mumbles Lifeboat, *Edward, Prince of Wales*, lost their lives attempting to rescue the crew of *S S Samtampa* and the window in All Saints Church is a memorial to the bravery of those men. The church overlooks the sea and is close to the lifeboat station. The design, a 'photomontage' of the scenes of that night, concentrates on the event in too much graphic detail. The imagery, which would have been appropriate for one of the town's secular buildings, fails to give the spiritual dimension to sacrifice, loss of life at sea, and bravery, needed in the church. The Christians' point of view is not paramount in the content of the work.

SAINT ANDREW'S CHURCH, PORTLAND

SOUTH AISLE WINDOW, 1981

ARTIST: JON CALLAN

Known locally as St Andrew's Avalanche Memorial Church, this small church on the Isle of Portland is a memorial to 106 men, women and children who lost their lives in the collision and shipwreck of the *Avalanche* and the *Forest* in 1877. To mark the centenary of the shipwreck and the church, stained glass was commissioned. The new glass is a new memorial to 106 people, symbolized by the lenses, and clearly portrays the sensation of a strong sea, ship with masts, yet in the composition there is a spiritual quality which allows the work a much wider interpretation; the meaning is not limited to the actual event.

'Initially I had thought of producing a traditional picture window, (the church already had several), but this idea wasn't really suitable. I wanted to produce a window that had a spiritual meaning to those who might interpret it that way, yet produce an object of beauty that could be contemplated and used to tell a story to those people who have no religious conviction. I wanted to maintain a harmony with the building and the existing work in the building'.

Jon Callan, Artist

SAINT GABRIEL'S CHURCH, BLACKBURN

BAPTISTRY WINDOW, 1977

ARTIST: BRIAN CLARKE

The architectually impressive St Gabriel's, Blackburn, was designed by F. X. Velarde and completed in 1933. It has been dramatically and unsympathetically altered in recent years, mainly due, it has to be said, to structural defects creating major problems. The external appearance has most dramatically changed, but the interior too has been altered. The reredos, original light fittings and stainless steel windows have all been replaced. However, the long tunnel nave with cream walls and simple fittings, many in chrome, retains much of the original atmosphere.

The two thin baptistry windows at the west end of the church and opposite the entrance are equally simple, and the stained glass fails to define the baptistry area adequately. The artist's idea of creating a 'no-mans land' in the central white area that fills nearly three-quarters of the window, and the small lump in the left hand window 'indicating art and philosophy breaking through into the mysterious world that exists between earth and heaven' have left a void area of no spiritual significance. This misses an opportunity to reassert the fundamental importance of baptism in Christian life. The artist's philosophical interpretation fails to be understood and mitigates against a spiritual understanding in the viewer.

BAR HILL (SHARED) CHURCH, CAMBRIDGE

CHAPEL WINDOW, 1972

ARTIST: RAY BRADLEY

Bar Hill is a new village outside Cambridge. The shared church is an inter-denominational building, doubling as a community centre. The community is a growing one and the chapel window in the church takes growth as its theme.

'The window depicts a plant-like form, slender at the base, but springing out to open and contain six "buds" representing the different denominations which share the church. The idea of the Christian community meeting face to face, accepting one another, growing together, is continued in the core of plant. The core then flows out across the whole window, the final explosion of growth, the flower of the plant, a complete fulfilment of the Christian life through the presence of God.

   This flower is basically purple to represent the mysteries of God with stamen-life forms expanding from the centre to delineate a cross and also suggest far-reaching influences, a lattice system super-intelligence, which reaching still upward disperses pollen or seeds, the promise of continuing growth and fertilization'.

Ray Bradley, Artist

PARISH CHURCH, LLANSAMET

SOUTH AISLE WINDOW, 1978

ARTIST: DAVID LEVERSHA

On my visit to Llansamlet Church, the incumbent referred me to Revelations, quoting 'Behold I make all things new' as an interpretation that he had placed upon this aisle window. He explained that the work symbolized to him the work of the Lower Swansea Valley Project which has sought to reclaim the derelict industrial valley below Llansamlet. Perhaps a strength of an abstract composition is that it can be open to many interpretations on many levels. Interpretations can also change with familiarity. A work of art should be like an old friend and surprise us from time to time by showing a new aspect of itself, and should never be taken for granted.

The artist comments on the design: 'My intention was to produce a curtain of soft, cool light where someone could sit quietly. This and colour harmony with the interior were my most important aims'.

David LeVersha, Artist

SAINT JOSEPH'S CHURCH, CRICKHOWELL

EAST WINDOW, 1978

ARTIST: DAVID PEARL

Saint Joseph's Church, Crickhowell is a small and simple church. The altar has an equally simple wooden framed window on either side and a small quatrefoil directly over. In 1978, new stained glass replaced the existing glass. Possessing a gentle light, these restrained windows are contemplative and unchallenging.

SAINT MARY'S CHURCH, SWANSEA

PAIR OF WINDOWS, WEST WALL, 1982

ARTIST: CATRIN JONES

The pair of west windows at St Mary's Church, Swansea, commemorate the marriage of Lady Diana Spencer with Prince Charles. It is entirely fitting that marriage is celebrated in colour in the church, symbols of love between two people.

'My primary instinct when designing with the thought of marriage in mind was to try to present the most basic rudiments of such an union. I think the most important themes in marriage are the spiritual union of two people before God and the continued fulfilment of their part in private life. I chose to represent the purity of spirit with the clarity of primary colour. The commitment of one person to another is depicted by the simple gesture of the joining of hands, an international statement of peace and unity. Flowers represent the joy of the occasion. The veil, a tangible link with the actual ceremony, unites the two windows'.

Catrin Jones, Artist

SAINT MARY'S CHURCH, SWANSEA

PAIR OF WINDOWS, NORTH AISLE, 1982

ARTIST: KUNI KAJIWARA

Two north aisle lights in St Mary's Church have been linked together on either side of a tall, bleak wooden memorial. The two windows relate Swansea's recent history; the destruction in the war, industry, choirs singing, the harbour. Higher up, there is an exciting, exuberant host of angels.

SAINT BARTHOLOMEW'S CHURCH, BATH

EAST WINDOW, 1980

ARCHITECT: JOHN VIVIAN

ARTIST: MARK ANGUS

The building of St Bartholomew's Church, Bath, started in 1936, was stopped in 1939, when only the nave was built. The church was bombed in the air raids on Bath, and rebuilt after the war. But it was not until 1979 that a decision was made to pierce the blank east wall to form an east window and complete the church. The architect, John Vivian, chose Mark Angus to execute the stained glass.

'The east window comprises a cross-shaped opening above the altar, and seven openings much higher up the wall. I immediately decided that the cross window was the focal point, perhaps the ultimate Christian symbol over the altar. I also decided not to design a crucifix, preferring to show an empty cross. The whole theme concentrates on the paradox of the pain and suffering of the cross and the reality of the resurrection. Symbols of the passion, the five wounds, the crown of thorns, etc., are surrounded by purple which symbolizes Christ's blood and the power of the Spirit — the resurrection implicit in the crucifixion. The purple is carried up to the seven higher lights; its acceptance into heaven'.

Mark Angus, Artist

'The stained glass has helped our whole concept of God and our worship. The content of the window is a means to an end; the congregation responding through the window to the purposes of God. Indeed, I invite them to enjoy the glass on a spiritual plane. We all see new meanings in the work, many not intended by the artist. For example, there is a gold band around the centre three top lights and I see this as a band of promise as a wedding ring, a covenant relationship. I don't see the work as "abstract", rather as having a concrete meaning with which, in a sense, we can have a relationship'.

Roger Hoare, Vicar

102

SAINT BARTHOLOMEW'S CHURCH, BATH

WEST WINDOWS, 1980, 1982

ARTIST: MARK ANGUS

'Fire and water are two basic elements to the Church: the water of baptism, and the Pentecostal flame. In a sense when we view the baptism window for example you say "Is that my experience of baptism in that I rose to receive the covenant relationship, the love of God through prayer?". In that way the window speaks of the love of God to us'.

Roger Hoare, Vicar

The first sight as one enters St Bartholomew's Church, Bath, is the glow of orange and red on the wall alongside the 'Fire' west window. Drawn towards the window one sees that the image is of a searing hot tongue of flame coming down from above, scorching the surface. The flame seems to be lighting the lenses below. There is a strong link made between this window and the lower part of the east window when one turns towards the altar.

The more subtle colours of the baptism window are seen as one leaves the church. The watery quality is apparent, but the motifs are ambiguous. In fact, the windows illustrate the rewards of baptism, the seven gifts of the spirit, ascension (the ladder motif), and in purple, the new church rising, not yet completed. Placing the new church in the baptism window can be seen as a simile for the new believer rising out of water because of God's promise.

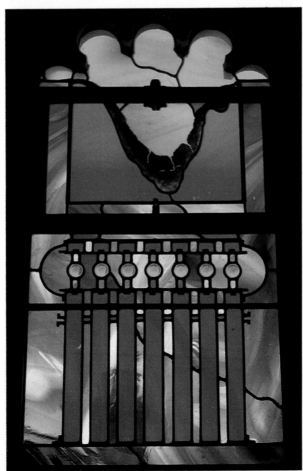

SAINT PETER'S CHURCH, WOLVERCOTE

SOUTH AISLE WINDOW, 1976

ARTIST: JOHN PIPER

The window takes as its theme a line from the Gospel of St John:

> 'They took branches of palm trees and went out to meet him'
> (John 12. 13)

All sorts of hands representing all sorts of people are waving palms energetically at Christ's triumphant entry into Jerusalem. The portrayal of the historical event thus has a contemporary relevance.

SELECTED GAZETTEER

SELECTED GAZETTEER

(*See list of illustrated works — page 32)

	AVON		
BATH	*St Stephen's Church	1982	Mark Angus
	*St Bartholomew's Church	1980	Mark Angus
		1981	(see frontispiece)
		1982	
BRISTOL	Bristol Cathedral	1965	Keith New
	Cathedral of St Peter & St Paul, Clifton		Henry Haig
	Clifton School Chapel	1964	Patrick Reyntians
	All Saints Church, Clifton	1967	John Piper
	Bristol Synagogue	1978	Mark Angus
	St Peter's, Henleaze	1967	Alan Younger
CLAVERTON	St Mary the Virgin	1983	Mark Angus
			(see page 14)
KEYNSHAM	*St Dunstan's Church	1979	Mark Angus
	BEDFORDSHIRE		
TOTTERNHOE	St Giles' Church	1970	John Piper
	BERKSHIRE		
READING	St Mathew's Church	1968	John Piper
SANDHURST	Royal Military Academy Chapel		Lawrence Lee
WINDSOR CASTLE	St George's Chapel	1969	John Piper
	BUCKINGHAMSHIRE		
ETON	Eton College Chapel	1952	Eve Hone
		1959–	John Piper
		1964	
			Moira Forsyth
BLEDLOW RIDGE	St Paul's Church	1968	John Piper
FAWLEY	St Mary's Church	1976	John Piper
FLACKWELL HEATH	Christ Church	1962	Patrick Reyntians
MILTON KEYNES	*Milton Keynes Crematorium Chapel	1982	Graham Pentelow
TURVILLE	St Mary's Church	1975	John Piper

111

	CAMBRIDGESHIRE		
BAR HILL	*Bar Hill Shared Church	1972	Ray Bradley
BABRAHAM	St Peter's Church	1968	John Piper
CAMBRIDGE	Churchill College Chapel	1970	John Piper
	*Robinson College Chapel	1978–1982	John Piper
	DERBYSHIRE		
BIRCHOVER	*Parish Church	1977	Brian Clarke
DERBY	Cathedral Church of All Saints	1964	Ceri Richards
	DEVON		
BUCKFASTLEIGH	Buckfast Abbey		Buckfast Monks
PLYMOUTH	St Andrew's Church	1957–1968	John Piper
TORQUAY	Central Church	1970	Peter Tysoe
	DORSET		
POOLE	Oratory School Chapel	1964	Patrick Reyntians
PORTLAND	St Andrew's Church	1981	Jon Callan
	DURHAM		
DURHAM	Durham Cathedral Galilee Chapel	1964	Alan Younger
	*Nave	1984	Mark Angus
	DYFED		
CARDIGAN	*Our Lady of the Taper	1980	Amber Hiscott
	ESSEX		
HORNCHURCH	*Church of the English Martyrs	1981	Goddard and Gibbs Studio
THUNDERSLEY	*Church of St Peter	1966	Ray Bradley
	GLOUCESTERSHIRE		
PRINKNASH	*Prinknash Abbey	1972	Brother Gilbert Taylor
	GLAMORGAN, MID		
CWMDÂR	St Luke's Church	1963	Timothy Lewis
	GLAMORGAN, SOUTH		
LLANDAFF	Llandaff Cathedral	1961	John Piper
	GLAMORGAN, WEST		
LLANSAMLET	*Parish Church	1978	David LeVersha
MUMBLES	*All Saints Church	1977	Timothy Lewis
SWANSEA	*St Mary's Church	1965 1981 1981	John Piper Kuni Kajiwara Catrin Jones

112

	GWENT		
NEWPORT	St Woolo's Cathedral	1964	*John Piper*
	HAMPSHIRE		
HINTON AMPNER	Parish Church	1970	*Patrick Reyntians*
HOUNDS	St Mary's Church	1962	*Patrick Reyntians*
ODIHAM	All Saints Church	1968	*Patrick Reyntians*
	HEREFORDSHIRE		
HEREFORD	St Barnabas's Church	1982	*David Morrish*
	HERTFORDSHIRE		
CUFFLEY	*St Andrew's Church	1965	*Whitefriars Studio*
		1978	*Chapel Studio*
WELWYN GARDEN CITY	St John's Church	1964	*Whitefriars Studio*
		1982	*Mike Davis*
	KENT		
CANTERBURY	Canterbury Cathedral South East Transept	1956	*Ervin Bossanyi*
MARDEN	St Michael and All Saints Church	1963	*Patrick Reyntians*
ORPINGTON	Christ Church	1976	*Ray Bradley*
TUDELEY	All Saints Church		*Marc Chagall*
TUNBRIDGE WELLS	Convent of the Sacred Heart		*Paul Quail*
			Keith New
	LANCASHIRE		
BLACKBURN	*St Gabriel's Church	1977	*Brian Clarke*
HABERGHAM	*All Saints Church	1976	*Brian Clarke*
LEYLAND	St Mary's Priory	1964	*Patrick Reyntians*
LONGRIDGE	*St Laurence's Church	1975	*Brian Clarke*
THORNTON-CLEVELEYS	Christ Church	1976	*Brian Clarke*
	LONDON, GREATER		
FULHAM	Charing Cross Hospital Chapel	1977	*John Piper*
EDMONTON	*St Edmund's Church	1982	*Mark Angus*
FULHAM	Oratory School Chapel	1970	*Patrick Reyntians*
HILLINGDON	*Hillingdon Hospital Chapel	1965	*Jane Gray*
TWICKENHAM	*St Margaret's Church	1968	*Patrick Reyntians*
SOUTHALL	St Anselm's Church	1971	*Patrick Reyntians*
WEST GREEN	Christ Church with St Peter	1982	*Ray Bradley*
WESTMINSTER	St Margaret's Church	1967	*John Piper*

	LINCOLNSHIRE		
LINCOLN	Lincoln Cathedral		*Geoffrey Clarke*
	WEST LOTHIAN		
EDINBURGH	Lansdowne School Chapel	1982	*Douglas Hogg*
	GREATER MANCHESTER		
MANCHESTER	*Manchester Cathedral	1964	*Margaret Traherne*
		1973	
		1976	*Anthony Holloway*
		1982	
	MERSEYSIDE		
LIVERPOOL	Cathedral of Christ the King — Lantern	1965–1967	*John Piper*
	— Chapel of the Blessed Sacrament	1967	*Ceri Richards*
	Lady Chapel and the Chapel of St Paul	1965	*Margaret Traherne*
	St Christopher's Grange	1970	*Patrick Reyntians*
	NORFOLK		
SCOLE	All Saints Church	1965	*Patrick Reyntians*
GRISTON	Wayland Prison Chapel	1983	*Mark Angus*
	NORTHAMPTONSHIRE		
ABINGTON	St Peter and St Paul's Church	1982	*John Piper*
HASELBECH	Parish Church		*Alan Younger*
OUNDLE	Oundle School Chapel	1954–1956	*John Piper*
WELLINGBOROUGH	All Hallows Church	1955	*Evie Hone*
		1962	*Jean Barillet*
		1961	
		1964	*John Piper*
		1969	
	NOTTINGHAMSHIRE		
HUCKNALL	Catholic Church	1961	*Patrick Reyntians*
MISTERTON	Parish Church	1966	*John Piper*
WOODTHORPE	Church of the Good Shepherd	1964	*Patrick Reyntians*
	OXFORDSHIRE		
NETTLEBED	*St Bartholomew's Church	1970	*John Piper*
		1976	
OXFORD	Nuffield College Chapel	1965	*John Piper*
PISHILL	St Paul's Church	1969	*John Piper*

114

SANDFORD ST MARTIN	St Martin's Church	1974	*John Piper*
WOLVERCOTE	*St Peter's Church	1976	*John Piper*
STAFFORDSHIRE			
WOLVERHAMPTON	*St Andrew's Church	1968	*John Piper*
BEDWORTH	Methodist Church	1979	*Paul Quail*
SOMERSET			
TAUNTON	All Saints Church		*Henry Haig*
EAST SUSSEX			
ST LEONARDS ON SEA	Parish Church	1957	*Patrick Reyntians*
WEST SUSSEX			
LOXWOOD	*St John the Baptist's Church	1980–1982	*Penelope Neave*
CHICHESTER	Chichester Cathedral	1978	*Marc Chagall*
SUFFOLK			
ALDEBURGH	*Church of St Peter and St Paul	1979	*John Piper*
POWYS			
CRICKHOWELL	*St Joseph's Church	1978	*David Pearl*
WARWICKSHIRE			
COVENTRY	Coventry Cathedral	1959–1962	*John Piper, Margaret Traherne, Lawrence Lee, Keith New, Geoffrey Clarke, Einar Forseth*
	*Church of the Sacred Heart	1979	*Goddard and Gibbs Studios*
WILTSHIRE			
SALISBURY	Salisbury Cathedral	1980	*Gabriel Loire*
YORKSHIRE			
AMPLEFORTH	Ampleforth Abbey	1963	*Patrick Reyntians*
KEIGHLEY	Malsis School Chapel	1967	*John Piper*
SHEFFIELD	St Mark's Church	1963	*John Piper*
YORK	York Minster Zouche Chapel		*Ervin Bossanyi*

BIBLIOGRAPHY

BIBLIOGRAPHY

ARCHER, Michael, *Stained Glass* (Pitkin Pictorials, 1979).

ARMITAGE, Liddall, *Stained Glass* (Leonard Hill, 1960)

BEYER, V. *Stained Glass Windows* (Oliver and Boyd, 1964)

CLARKE, Brian (Editor), *Architectural Stained Glass* (John Murray, 1979)

CHAGALL, Marc, *The Jerusalem Windows* (New York Arts, 1962)

DAY, Michael, *Modern Art in Church* (Royal College of Art Paper No. 12, 1982)

ELSKUS, Albinas, *The Art of Painting on Glass* (Routledge and Kegan Paul, 1981)

GLASS/LIGHT. Exhibition Catalogue (Thorn Lighting, 1978)

GLASS MASTERS. Contemporary Stained Glass from West Germany Exhibition Catalogue (Welsh Arts Council, 1980)

HAYES, Dagmar, *Ervin Bossanyi: The Splendour of Stained Glass* (Friends of Canterbury Cathedral, 1965)

HENZE, Anton, and Theodor Fitthaut, *Contemporary Church Art* (Sheed and Ward, 1956)

HILL, HILL, HALBERSTADT, *Stained Glass, Music for the Eye.* (The Scrimshaw Press, 1976)

HOFSTATTER, Hans, H. *Johannes Schreiter, Neue Glasbilder* (Heinz Moos, 1965)

LEE, Lawrence, *The Appreciation of Stained Glass* (Oxford University Press, 1977)

LEE, Lawrence, *Stained Glass* (Oxford Paperbacks, 1967)

LEE, Lawrence, George Seddon and Francis Stephens, *Stained Glass* (Mitchell Beazley, 1976)

MARTEAU, R, *The Stained Glass Windows of Chagall, 1957–1970 (1973)*

McCLINTON, Katharine Morrison, *Christian Church Art Through the Ages* (Macmillan, 1962)

MEINSTERMANN, George, *Die Fenster der Feldkirche* (Galerie Heinemann, 1981)

MILLS, Edward. D. *The Modern Church* (The Architectural Press, 1956)

NEW BRITISH GLASS, Exhibition Catalogue (Centre International du Vitrail, 1982)

NEWTON, Eric, William Neil, *The Christian Faith in Art* (Hodder and Stoughton, 1966)

OSBORNE, June, *Stained Glass in England* (Frederick Muller, 1981)

PFAFF, Konrad, *Ludwig Schaffrath* (Scherpe, 1977)

PIPER, John, *Stained Glass: Art or Anti-Art* (Studio Vista, 1968)

PIPER, John, *Painting in Coloured Light* Exhibition Catalogue (Kettles Yard Gallery, 1982)

PROPHECY AND VISION, Exhibition Catalogue (Editors Peter Burman and Fr Kenneth Nugent, 1982)

REYNTIANS, Patrick, *The Technique of Stained Glass* (Batsford, 1967)

RAMANAUSKAITE, Luidvika, *Modern Lithuanian Stained Glass* (Aurora Art Publishers, 1979)

SOWERS, Robert, *The Lost Art* (Zwemmer, 1954)

SOWERS, Robert, *Stained Glass: An Architectural Art* (Zwemmer, 1965)

SPENCE, Basil, *Phoenix at Coventry* (Geoffrey Bles, 1962)

STEPHANY, Erich and others, *Licht Glas Farbe* (M. Brimberg, 1983)

THOMAS, Brian, *Directory of the British Society of Master Glass Painters* (Oriel Press, 1972)